THE RAM

Contents

4 MASTERPIECE

5 THE RAMPAGE

I   THE WALL

The Wall in the Corner by the Stairs

The wall
covered with the stucco
of oblivion,
a bit slanted,
somewhat invisible
to the glassy eye
of the mundane.

Coarse plaster,
a vertical burying ground of rhizopods,
grains of sand
from Mathias Braun, Baroque sculptor, and
husks of Celtic germs.

A thin coat of latex paint and a cobweb,
a laurel wreath
on the neck of last year's gnat
trembling in the draft
like a mummy of our
forever distant
love for Helen of Troy.

A crack like
a barge-puller's dried-up river,
a hole left by a nail,
the mouth of the volcano
Empedocles jumped into,
big as a sigh,
the hollow brain of a mite,
the little mouth of a prince

open in wonder
at the empty-handedness
of our memory.

Paintings on walls.
Saroyan in a frame. Beckett in a frame.
Brueghel in a frame.
Mummy, when she was twenty, framed,
me, when I was six, framed,

all
dead
for ages.

All identical with the wall.

Home

At the tip of the needle.

In the eye of a virtual tornado.

In Pilsen, in San Francisco.

In the nervous nest, decaying
in the poem, in the firing
of neurons.

In a cobweb. In the field of vision.

In the deafening polar province
called You.

At the rim of a disc
underneath which there's only
the spasmodic starry firmament
and the mute nonsense
known as Eternity.

Love, as They Say

Days and nights take turns, minute by minute.
Central Park spins round,
the collector jumps on the platform
of the merry-go-round and collects
tickets from water-nymphs and horses.
That doesn't concern us.

Behind glass, stick insects mate,
and she is devouring his head,
he doesn't need it for mating anyway.

The key fits in the lock,
a molecule fits in a molecule,
John the Baptist baptizes as usual,
averting his gaze.

For us, the Exodus from Egypt
begins again. For us this is
the advent of invisibility,
the night of glowing strawberries,
the sepia darkness undersea
with a single warm tentacle.

For us, this is the cover
of a book without letters or pictures,
the contents to follow later,
it is – as always – for the first time in history,
for the last time in the history of skin,
the last time in the history of parchment,
like the tale of the unborn swineherds,

the under-the-altar sacrament, still unknown,
with the eternal light
turned all the way up.

This is the only extraterrestrial thing
left to us.

Like the victorious palpitation of silky wings
on the temporary tombs – of butterflies,
and of stick insects with chitinous vaginas.

Duties of One Who Left

Although
the nest was windward and
the River Thames or the River Shelda
rolled its waves below

although
it took our voices
five or fifty minutes to turn orange
and interfere according to
the Doppler principle,

although your body
sprang up from a wondrous fantasy
by Brueghel, Titian and Miró

I left you
to see what not leaving was like,
and to miss it,

to see
that on the green late-afternoon soccer pitch
a lone child rides a lone bike
and across the western sky runs the word Offside

and that every angel
by himself
is terrible.

Whale Songs

At two o'clock in the morning
I hear my mitral valve
from the depth of the dim, blood-filled tunnel
which is me. Cellular receptors
fit with a metallic click
into the locks
and the cells are me and the locks are me.
From some symphonic distance
there sounds the song of the whales,
and it contains me.

In some black castle
Sleeping Beauty has pricked herself on a thorn,
which is me. The clock has stopped
– in our house clocks stop at any moment
because she will prick herself at any moment,
on a tiny crock shard,
on a word,
on a milk tooth,
on a toy that has fallen into the gutter –
and so there's a still life, *nature morte*,
with me in the genetic background.

A paper kite stiffens in the air,
and yet, Einstein says, Time is always going, but never gone,
and yet, my mother says, ten years after her death,
Oh yes, oh yes,
and a clock starts again,

the Invisible passes through the room like a ball of lightning,
Sleeping Beauty lays eggs full of little spiders,
the whales re-enter the tunnel

and I start again
being the machine
for the production
of myself.

My Mother Learns Spanish

She started at the age
of eighty-two. She falls asleep
each time, page 26.
Algo se trama.

The pencil that underlines verbs
sets out on the page reluctantly
tracing the delicate outlines
of death.
No hay necesidad de respuestas.

It draws the routes
of Hernan Cortez's expeditions.
It draws El Greco's eye.
It draws Picasso's fish,
too big for its own aquarium.

A pencil as stubborn
as Fuente Ovejuna.
As the bull in the arena
Placa de Toros Monumental,
already on its knees
while horses wait
to drag away its body.

No hay necesidad de respuestas,
no answers are needed.
Now or ever.
She sleeps
ever
now.

While Gaudi
as if in homage
never completes
his cathedral,
Sagrada Familia.

Anatomy of January

On the carpal bones
metacarpal bones with dwindling cartilage,
the ulna
like a ruler for parakeets.

A string is attached to the joint,
a string that goes over the horizon,
southwest.

Rooks are falling from the sky,
under oath.

Anatomy of September

Not yet.

In the submarine gardens the sea-grasses
still wave.
In the sky the biplane of the jugglers
still holds on
by its fingernails.

In the blue room, on uneven tracks,
a toy train circles incessantly,
driven by a spring

and with no destination.

Anatomy of November

When we wake
there will be a leg missing
or an eye,
or a finger, the dainty ring finger.

At some distance
your royal smile will shine.
You will flow over me
like the southern sea,
like the blood
in a coronary bypass,

carrying away whatever remains.

Apollo's arrows
will ripple through the liquid air.

When we wake,
we will be only you,
smiling like Niobe.

The End of the Week

Of course it's all based
on a timetable, sometimes valid
Monday to Friday, sometimes on Saturday,
very rarely on Sunday (when He rested
from all His labours),

and we carry it in a forgotten pocket
so we usually miss the train.

But we'll get there anyway.

It will be Sunday again, the day of withered songs.
On the first floor, by the window without curtains,
a little girl in a red dress will stand
and wait.

In the Spanish square they'll be burning
eighteen Jewish Marranos
in honour of the wedding of Maria Luisa and Carlos.

But we won't even stop
and will go home by a back way,
deep in thought.

The Day of the Pollyanna

The dough didn't rise that day.
The kitchen clock stopped.
Against all hope
the streetcar turned around
at the Slovany terminal
and started back.

But in the second car,
at the very back, a little girl
wearing a big blue woollen cap,
sat holding a doll
that resembled a three-month-old
tapir fetus,
and sang, in an antimony voice,

Don't cry ... don't cry ... don't cry.

Though nobody felt like crying,
tapirs least of all.

2 FREEDOM

Freedom

At a dizzying height
on the skyscraper's wall
a sky-blue flag.

Down the middle of the street
a polio-stricken boy
roller-skating,
passes spasmodically,

pushing himself ahead
with just one foot,
the one that isn't
wearing a brace.

Scene with Fiddlers

It snowed from the heart. And for years.

On we went, the clarinet an icicle,
the fiddle shivering under the coat. It was getting dark
in a gaping landscape. Beyond the hill
some pig, in mortal agony. No trace of music,
only silence, thickening.

All our life
we'd been struggling through snowdrifts,
from stage left to stage right.

And at the very end,
as we were breathless, thoughtless,
and therefore weightless,
in all that silence
somebody tootled.

Toot, an ember of music. Toot,
music itself.

So that the road, the snow,
the scene and the silence
could be
'subtracted from eternity'.*

*Jaroslav Seifert

At Last

At last we were masters of our heads,
masters of the city,
masters of our shadows
and our equinox.

Someone fired a shot to celebrate,
but only the kind with a cork
tied to a string.

And then we opened the cages
and ferrets ran out.
Out of the skull ran brown and white
spotted rats.
Out of the heart flew
blood-soaked cuckoos.

Out of the lungs
a condor rose, croaking with rage
because of the way his plumes had been squashed
in the bronchi.

Even a panther showed up,
on the loose from an obsolete circus,
starved, ready to eat
even the Emperor Claudius.

You could hear squeaks in the streets –
the groans and shouts
of expiring fiends.

And at last we were masters
of our new moon.

But we couldn't step out
of our doorways;
someone might cast
a spell on us.

We might even
be hostage
to ourselves.

The Moth

The moth,
having left its pupa
in the galaxy
of flour grains
and pots of rancid dripping,

the moth
discovers in this
topical darkness
that it's a kind of butterfly
but
it can't believe it,
it can't believe it,

it can't believe
that it's a tiny,
flying, relatively
free moth

and it wants to go back,
but there's no way.

Freedom makes
the moth tremble
for ever. That is,
twenty-two hours.

Crowd-Walkers

They get up early,
the new epoch has scarcely dawned,
people are rubbing bloodshot eyes
and speech still catches against
the emery-board of the unusual,
but they are here already
stamping on the heads of crowds,
their horny hoofs booming inside the skulls,
and they're already preaching eternal truths
out of their horsey mouths,
and already the shaking hands
pour out from their sleeves.

Trough-centaurs.
Always right there, gobbling it up.

And while people are still replaying
yesterday's play in their heads,
these folks already know
that Lear never should have been king,
Polonius didn't belong behind that arras,
Romeo should have been Juliet,

that we were all miscast.

Across our heads they trample to the stage,
pull out the harness and tack
and start their *Richard the Third*.

Hoofs were here before Shakespeare.

The Earth Is Shrinking

The earth is shrinking,
there's
almost no place to set a flowerpot.
And rain-worms get confused
and intertwine
in knots
like fibrillary tangles
in the brain
of a slightly crazy
temple dancer.

The earth is shrinking.
Maybe
due to the evaporation
of good intentions.
Maybe
due to the lifting
of a baldachin
over the head
of a saintly
marsupial.

Certainly
due to the dead
devouring the earth.
For a hundred thousand years
the dead have been settled in,
packed down, eating earth

and excreting marsupial
good intentions.

While Fleeing

It was Rembrandt
or Poincaré,
or Einstein,
or Prokofiev,
two years old,
and his mother
was shot
or buried
in rubble
while fleeing,
and she was pressing him
to her breast
when she fell,
he was smothered,
and disappeared without having appeared.

When we find
small white stones
or a certain yellow pebble,
we play with them,
we put them together
to form little piles,
letters,
and circles.

It may be an
unconscious
burial rite
for times when
there aren't any

passage graves,
cremation sites,
bronze clasps,

when only
a couple of million
mothers flee
constantly flee
from somewhere to
somewhere
else.

The Journey

On the horizontal plane
cities pass
like sensors for signals
from elsewhere.

Less and less I understand
precisely why I'm here and whether
it's the right me.

Each railway station and bus terminal
has its photographs of missing children:

    Christopher Milton Dansky
    Abducted by unknown individual
    DOB: 3/30/87
    Eyes: brown
    Height: 2'6"
    Weight: 30lbs
    Hair: black
    Last seen: 5/18/89

    Jennifer Chia ...
    ... seen 10/18/89

They still smile from their photographs
at all the terminals,
although they know by now precisely
why they are not right here,
not their right selves, and

the Queen of the Undead
hangs on their lips
like a weasel

and a trickle of blood runs down
their chins to patter
gently, drop by drop,
on a blue and white toy drum
bought at a street fair. And in a soft
and cosmic darkness
mama is teaching fledgling vampires
how to fly.

On a bench, under the photographs,
a mildly crazy codger
sings in a raspy voice
like the King of Legoland.

Not-so-brief Reflection on the Edict

The Edict, possibly Diocletian's,
displayed in the marketplace at Aizanoi in 291,
states in letters engraved on stone:

Man, 16 to 40 years	30,000 denarii
Woman, same age	25,000 denarii
Homo (man) ab annis LX superius	
et VIII inferius	15,000 denarii
Mulier (woman) ab annis "	10,000 denarii
Riding horse	100,000 denarii
Equus militaris primae formae	36,000 denarii
Dromedairus optimus	20,000 denarii
Vacca (cow) primae formae	2,000 denarii
Capra (goat) primae formae	600 denarii

These prices are hard to beat,
for a military horse three girls up to eight years
and ten good goats is certainly not excessive,
anyway, girls, who knows what they get up to,

and for two men in the productive age range
three dromedaries are a bargain,
they're a lot less expensive to feed,
if need be they can even drink their own urine

and these days who would offer almost seven oldsters
for a trained full-blooded stallion? –
someone like Richard the Third, perhaps,
but only in special circumstances,

today for the murder of, say, a creditor, one pays
less than for a Mercedes 230,
and a football player primae formae
is worth about a pound of gold, that was 72,000 denarii

and it would take a superspy,
with a price on his head, to equal
the value of eight little elementary schoolboys
or a herd of Phrygian cows of the Friesian breed.

A herd of girls can make, in a month on the street,
only about the equivalent of a two-humped camel
which was 60,000 ... No way, Diocletian's prices
were reasonable and, when you think of it, very clearly stated.

Of course it's appalling to sell slaves in a market,
even if, here and there, in one of the planet's blind spots,
the earth swells because it bears
thousands of priceless yellow, black and white bloody heads,
and kwashiorkor bellies like rosary beads

which lead to the absolute of the heavenly cafeterias,
as well as fingers wriggling out of glassy pupae,
finger after finger, with crumpled nails,
like eczematous sphinx moths, irreversible hands,

that grope on plains where armless philosophers
graze flocks of cotton-wool tampons,
and where it isn't so much about the blood,
it's more about the cellulose.

The hands grope, they fold into fists,
turning to jelly in their final moments,

till nothing remains for philosophy,
nor for the emperor, nor for ice cream.

Of course it's appalling to sell people in a market,
even if the poet, furious, recites his prices
for right-coiling metaphysical shells,
for gnomic gooey gowns,

vesting the tepid volcanic depths
where even a pubic bone would perish,
although the poet dreams of self-generating genitals
strewn in the woods like morel mushrooms.

And poetry then resembles
a hundred and fifty cats' eyes,
pickled in vinegar in order
to see immortality.

Of course it's appalling to assess people in a market,
even if Dante's *Inferno* is measured in degrees centrigrade,
even if Sisyphus' labor is calculated in kilojoules,
and Diocletian's pressure on his pedestal in newtons,

even if we all write
our small daily edicts
on the night-time marketplace,
in the mid-morning home,

in the permanent grotto
of our genome.

The Goddess of Victory

Nike of Samothrace
used to be small
with a pox-scarred face
and a rag in her hand for mopping blood.

A deserter from the War of the Frogs and the Mice.

She crossed the pasture of black and white cows,
sinking into the ground.

She started to grow by yearning,
losing her head from fatigue and gaining a halo.

Her hands dropped off by themselves on the day
her wings appeared.

She was overwhelmed
by the pain of phantom limbs.

Now, in the Louvre,
she commands the stairs going up,
and, to the sound of Ravel's *Bolero*,
she paces on the spot like a radiant white matador
who killed the last bull
in the last corrida of heaven.

3 THE PIED PIPERS

The Pied Pipers

Dreams have reproduced until
you can't even move in your bed.
And in the library, books give birth to booklets
without any fertilization.

But outside, from the dark, there comes
a kind of tune, as though from ants,
yes, it's coming nearer, maybe a flute,
a catchy melody, sweet, diabetic,
and another and another,

intertwining like an Easter braid,
like snakes, each with two penises,
one with the other in its mandibles,
suggesting that hell and purgatory
and even illegal rubbish dumps
have been shut down,

that instead of information
there's only going to be Truth,

and the lyrical snout of the town
gapes with expectation
and on the gallstone pavements
skinny, grubby, scraggly-bearded
Pied Pipers with backpacks
lead their processions from the river

back

to the marketplace, to halls, to palaces,
(to cottages), pitiful Pied Pipers,
friends of rats and kids,

it's like the procession
of a whole brigade
of under-age saviours
(mother waits behind the steering wheel
of night's black limousine),

and it marches to the bed,
it marches into the library,

the truth swelling like a pot of porridge,

long threads of language
hang from the Pipers' pipes
like spit, the truth puffs up
in our homes like a cuckoo's egg

and instead of molecular darkness
there's a sudden yellow-brown
as if pus were getting pregnant:

the Pied Pipers' roads in Siebenburgen Land
are lined with boils
that burst, one after the other
while the truth howls and trumpets,
like a dead driver, slumped against his car-horn,

'nothing but' overwhelms us.

Which may be the salvation they've been preaching.

Aloof

Only for highbrow men
and hysterical ladies:

An honest green water sprite
changes into a dapple-grey
dripping with tassels,
philosophical headcheese, with parsley,
nests in the mind,
a manic-depressive tapeworm
secretes abundant word-mucus.

The self expands like
an elastic wart, swells like
a cattle tick
pumped with paradise gas,
and it doesn't want to know
anything,
it will simply shine from the snout
a golden tooth
during the dusk of iguanas.

In a barred chamber
on web-draped walls
the coffee dregs mount
the oriental silence of being deepens
and the only human drama
is premature ejaculation.

A Moravian Castle

And by night
a ten-point stag
slinks through the corridors,
searching for his head
among the trophies,

as if a head could still belong
to anybody

in this age
of intestines.

Pompeii

In Pompeii
on paved and clattering
Venus Street
in full ancient sun
Little Red Riding Hood
drags her gift basket.

Such a beautiful moment.

Granny has
genital herpes, but
she doesn't know what that is.

Cholera is baked
in the pie.
But centurions
don't believe in infections.

Such beautiful times.

In the distance
Mount Vesuvius groans and gas
burns,
but geology
ended with Empedocles
in the mouth of Mount Etna.

Such a perfect epoch.

The glow-worm 'gins to pale
his uneffectual fire.
Soon
everyone will be baked
in the stony mud
like raisins of immortality,

and during excavations echoes will resound
of wolf chorales, Hamlet chorales, concubine chorales
about the good old days.

The British Museum

According to the rules of the fugue,
any ark
will be ruined
once, the trilingual
Rosetta Stone will be broken, stelae of Halicarnassus
will turn to dust, sandstone Assyrian spirits
with eagle heads will shyly take off,
the carved man-head lions of Ashur will croak,
the last red-granite hand of the Colossus of Thebes
will drop off, the Indian supergod Harikaru
will cover his onyx eyes, the mathematical scrolls
will catch fire, the pendant Zen poems will evaporate,
and the green hellish judge from the Ming dynasty will whine.

For the time of stone is meted out
and so is the time of myth.

Only genes are eternal,
from body to body,
from one breed to another breed,
on Southampton Row
in fact
you find walking genetic codes of Egyptian mummies,
deoxyribonucleic acid of the man from Gebelin,
hereditary traits of the man from Lindow,
whose earthly remains, cut in half by a bulldozer,
successfully swell under a glass bell,
in Bloomsbury, in fact, you find
all the eternity of the world rushing around
buying black flowers

for the Last Judgment, less Last
than a midnight hotdog.

So the British Museum is not to be found
in the British Museum.

The British Museum is in us,
in our very hearts,
in our very depths.

The Ten Commandments

And what are these commandments
right here, right now?

Moses in the form of an old drug addict
with a massive sticky beard,
his whole body changed into soul, but it stinks
a little,
his overcoat like a Babylonian dung heap,
he sleeps in the morning rays of the leftover sun
in the entryway of a theatre on the Strand,
dreams like rolls of barbed wire,
zippered-up dreams, like the mating of centipedes,
dreams like wings growing on man
just before the abyss,

like when you turn the computer off
and forget to save your work,
like when the Lord of multitudes
flees the multitudes.

All the wisdom of the world is in his bag, worn
as the stomach wall of a camel from Canaan,
like the dura mater of an anencephalic,
hundreds of frayed rolls
of old newspapers held with rubber bands,
everything that happened over the last ten years
set in the alphabet of the dermestes beetle.

And what *are* these commandments?
One should ask Moses, the ram with curly horns,
stinking at the head of the herd, in the doorway of the theatre,

and he is asked (silently) by thousands of mid-morning sheep,
chewing, scribbled over with eight-point type,
sexual sheep of foam rubber,
commercial sheep of brown polyethylene,
lambs of frayed denim,
tourist lambs with Baedeker erections,
apostolic herds of mutton with azure-blue parasols,
coming down from heaven in gas-guzzling
chariots, greased with Johnson's wax.

And he is going to preach the ten commandments ten times for
   ten pence,
the ten commandments as ten mutations of the virus
of immunodeficiency,
as ten gulps from a goatskin bag,
with the last breath.

And in fact the ten commandments will be
ten times why – and therefore for nothing
at the very end of the magnetic tape
stretching along an inclined plane
around the world
and back.

Literary Bash

Like eggs of hail
from the blue sky,
the buzz of greasy bluebottles,
the twitter of eggheads.

Interior sounds
of matter fatigue.

Never stopping.

But even Orpheus
when things got tough
and he was leading Eurydice
out of the underworld
was quiet as a grave,
the only sound
his crunching step
on the bodies of snails
shedding indigo blood.

In our world-under-the-world
there will be no Eurydice,
just the gabble of tipsy
bickering words.

The Autumn Orchard

Some pawky,
black apple
executed on a naked twig.

Two pigeons
on a rundown fence
tearing white feathers from themselves
because there's nothing else
worth sorting.

Cinderella has smeared her body
with ashes, trying
to discourage
her father's incest.

Through an open window
a bunch of poets
are cursing violently.

Although, in fact, everything's
just the way they like it.

Universe of the Mouse

Amphora of darkness, Hittite grain
still fertile, black background music
of the earth. Cathedral marked by urine.
Memorial droppings like elementary particles.

The heart beats from fright to fright.

Inside, small armoured worms
and mutations of chromosome 11.
Well above the chorus of bats,
some Jupiter, four-legged, foggy,
the cogwheel of certitude.

He will not suffer our delicate fur to shed,
He will not suffer our spines to snap.
And when our Gracious Lady teeth
grind in the negligible second
of our death

and our small sooty eye, like
the dull eyeball of a crucified man,
mirrors Primeval Sludge, Eternal Dormition,

in a solemn voice He will answer a question
that nobody asked.

4 MASTERPIECE

Masterpiece

The only masterpiece
I ever created
was a picture of the moth Thysania agrippina
in pastel on gray paper.

Because I was never
much good at painting. The essence of art
is that we aren't very good at it.

The moth Thysania agrippina
rose from the stiff gray paper
with outstretched, comb-like antennae,

with a plush bottom resembling the buttocks
of the pigwidgeons of Hieronymus Bosch,
with thin legs on a shrunken chest
like those on Brueghel's grotesque figures
in *Dulle Griet*, it turned into Dulle Griet
with a bundle of pots and pans in her bony hand,

it turned into Bodhiddharma
with long sleeves,

it was Ying or Shade
and Yang or Light, Chwei or Darkness
and Ming or Glow, it had
the black color of water, the ochre color of earth,
the blue color of wood,

I was as proud of it as an Antwerp councillor
or the Tenth Patriarch from the Yellow River,

I sprinkled it with shellac, which is
the oath that painters swear on Goethe's Science of Colors,

and then the art teacher took it to his study

and I forgot all about it

the way Granny used to forget
her dentures in a glass.

Ganesha

Siva the god was such a hothead.

When his little son bugged him in the bath,
he chopped his head off. Then
he had second thoughts, the way
supernaturals usually do,
and provided his son, Ganesha,
with the head of a baby elephant,
executed *ad hoc*.

So that Ganesha was the first transplant patient.
So that the rest of the elephant
vanished from history.

So that Ganesha made a nice living
as a monster. He rides on a rat
and visits us at Christmas,
asking what kind of Siva
has chopped off
our heads
this year.

The Earliest Angels

The first angels were swarthy, stooped,
hairy, with sloping foreheads
and crested skulls,
arms down to their knees. In place of wings
they had two parachutes of skin,
a species of black flying squirrel
in the volcanic winds.

Totally trustworthy.
They performed astounding miracles.
Transubstantiations. Metamorphoses
of mud into mudfish.
A rocking horse
inflated to heavenly size,
atomic fusion at room temperature,
the mirror held up to the spectator,
stirrings of consciousness
conceiving the majesty of death.

They worked hard.
They tinkered with graves.
They swam in murky waters.
They huddled in oviducts.
They hid behind the door.
They waited.
                    They waited in vain.

Resurrecting

By midnight
the vampires will appear, without ears, with tentacles,
fangs protruding,
and among them a well-groomed TV show host.

And the tombs will open, mummies
scraping across the thresholds, skeletons
swaying their legs on the churchyard walls,
prophets and witches will rise,
eunuchs and dukes, unbaptized babies,
serfs and suicides.

For every three, one purgatorial camera-man,
because you need a recording
for a really sexy metaphysics ...

Everyone will re-enact
the big moment:
the leap from the fifth floor
will be shot by the miniature guardian angel
who resembles a vigilant flying fish,

the vehmic murder will be captured by
an armoured lizard with four Agfa eyes,
the sadistic sex performance of a Chinese cook
with a Polish nun by a black Betamax monk,
who closely resembles a mole cricket.

Van Gogh's ear
will be recorded at the cut plane
by a fiddler crab
with a bifocal microscope.

The autumn battle of sad kings
by a golden-yellow wooden-legged saint,
The Love of Three Oranges
by a celluloid video virgin.

It will be eternity turned inside out,
the world throwing up, broadcast live,
mirroring in the eye of a blind god,
the scream of futility,
which, up to now, hasn't realized
even that it exists.

Anything about God

On a hill, Cezava,
in the heart of Europe
– the bones of a girl and a young man
from the Bronze Age,
without arms, without feet,
victims of ritual cannibalism.

And here are the varicose veins of the stone,
the last thing they saw
as their thoraxes were being opened,
with torrents of blood,
with a divine roar
and animal defecation.

And here is the vehement, variegated
silence of the soil.

As the master remarked,
whatever you say about God,
it's wrong.

The Statue of the Master

Inside
not even the twisting
– hair of the Gorgon Medusa –
not even the twisting intestines,

not even the swinging
– a Montgolfier in November –
not even the rising and sinking lungs,

not even the caramel-like
– a silent sweet-shop made of aluminum foil –
not even the caramel brain.

Not even the weight-lifting
– the solid, eternal Atlas –
not even the unremitting heart.

Inside
only stone
and stone
and stone

and it stands in the frost,
lips firmly compressed,

and swallows blood.

The Teaching of the Master

He spoke
and the shirts of penitents
fell to the ground, impregnated.

It was the Caesarian section of thought,
plush dolls were born, jubilating.
It was a profile of Everyman,
cut from black paper.
Ladybirds crawled out from under our fingernails.
Trumpets were heard at the walls of Jericho.
Our genes sizzled.

It was magnificent, as he spoke.
It's just that I can't recall
what he was talking about.

Elementary School Field Trip to
the Dinosaur Exhibit

Jurassic
roar.

Answered by
St Georges
or Rambos.

Only one
glum little boy,
evidently blind,
is lifted to the Triceratops
to breathlessly run his hand
up and down the skull,
over the bony collar,
the horns above the eyes,
the skin-folds on the neck,

the boy's face
is insanely blank,
but the hand already knows
that nothing is in the mind
that hasn't been in the senses,
that giants are pinkish-gray
like Handel's Concerto Grosso, Opus 6,
that life is just a step ahead
just like mother
always said.

Triceratops,
Abel's younger brother.

Dark in there, in
the midbrain:
the last dinosaur
meeting the last man.

The Darkness

Darkness, the electric eel, darkness, the throat of an alligator. Darkness is transformed into heat, time is expanded forwards and backwards, and in the circular tunnel our thought-protons accelerate. The autopsy is underway, the one conducted by antipodes. They have the faces of apes.

From the darkness comes a voice of unknown origins, foreign or our own, saying – You are getting on my nerves.

In the darkness, in our retinas, a puppet theatre is performing, without a stage manager. We have some characters in common. The demons, for instance.

The Silence

A broad smile from the abyss. A volcano that didn't erupt. The cannon ball, stalled above the turquoise landscape. Postponement of the punitive expedition. The Trojan War does not take place. Helen still waits for her orgasm. Laurel rots midway between defeat and victory.

Breathless, we have been wrapped by a boa constrictor, we have been squeezed by a blindworm, we have been fondled by a tapeworm, pinworms have hugged our vessels' endothelium, resulting in elephantiasis of our redundant limbs.

Fumes rise from the entrails of gutted orators. White teeth are strewn around, the result of a panel discussion and as a rudiment of reason. And the dead stroll among us, with life on the tip of their tongues.

5 THE RAMPAGE

The Rampage

The last time
there was a genuine rampage,
herds stampeding
with the zest of hurricanes,
with the pulsations of a storm,
and the force of destiny,

when the roar went up
against the villous ceiling,
when the stronger ones
pushed forward to the cruel
thunder of whips while the zombies
fell back into permanent darkness,

the last time
the cavalry charged
across the whole width of the enemy line
into the gap between life and death,
and not even one single droplet of misery
dripped,

the last time
something really won
and the rest turned into compost

that was when the sperm
made the journey
up the oviduct.

This was 'to be or not to be'.

Since that time we've been tottering round
with the embarrassment of softening skeletons,
with the wistful caution
of mountain gorillas in the rain;
we keep hoping for the time-lapse soul,
secreting
marital problems and
a stationary home metaphysics

against which
the adenosine triphosphate of every fucked-up cell
is like the explosion of a star
in a chicken coop.

Head-Smashed-In

Orpheus touches the strings of his lyre,
the leopard lies down with the lamb,
the hare with the wolf,
narwhal with herring,
Eurydice wades gratuitously
with silver lamé ankles
in the nebulous endothelium
of heart vessels,
all of this rendered
in drypoint etchings or aquatints –
life's great unity

and

the United Nations has designated
the cliff in Alberta called Head-Smashed-In
as a World Cultural Heritage Site,
the cliff where, for six thousand years,
Indians stampeded buffalo herds
into the gorge
and finished them off at the bottom
(the bloody mass of hides,
horror, hooves and horns,
roaring and bulging eye-balls)
in order to have enough meat.

So that

for six thousand years
Orpheus bangs the strings,
blood coagulates,
brain tissue softens and splinters,
the world cultural heritage
emanates sweet odours,
hysterics cluster at the altars

and

the heads of buffaloes
are still smashed in.

The Slaughterhouse

God is in the detail.
The god of blood is in
the heme molecule.

The gelid god Thanatos
is the microscopic whisper
in the brain stem –
and the transcendental tremble
of flesh
follows.

The god of calves
is the god of steaks and cutlets.

Over the red brick sheds
containing
the comprehensive roar of the world,

in the stinking azure sky,
a rope-walker balances
always pondering
just the next short step.

Anatomy of July

By the black water sits Gottfried Benn

who watches the circles where they drowned
the godless rat who spent
a beautiful childhood
in the entrails of the dead girl
found in the reeds.

By the golden water sits
the pious rat Ted
who watches the circles
still waiting.

Anatomy of December

Cracking of vertebrae.

Stooping, we compete
frenetically, at the paralympiad
of benefactors,
in calcium metabolism.

And lo, in the ion channel
a little candle. *And lo*,
the humped saint *saw*,

and behold, it *was very good.*

Anencephaly

(Newborn without a brain)

And Jonah was in the belly of the fish
three days and three nights.
And what kind of Jonah?

This one reclines in a cot on the ward,
has the face of a pink toad
and instead of a skull

                 a bag,

                        a limp red bag,
pulsating on the pillow.

His mouth-opening forms at times
a short proboscis
like a tapir searching in bamboo
for Saint Anthony.

And Erato the muse howls with sorrow in the elevator.

But he is brotherly, he is close
to Nature,

         to cauliflower,

                 to porcupines,
he is genuine, more genuine
than Broca's brain and Kant's reason,

he is innocent, more innocent
than Noah's offspring in the land of Shinar,

Bergson's seventh reincarnation,
or a surrealist's daydream.
And what kind of surrealist?

He drinks and excretes,
as decreed by the laws of Mother Earth.
Only a couple
                 of tainted genes too many
only a couple
                 of vile enzymes behind the poem,

a tiny avant-garde miracle.
And *who would first cast a stone*?

Perhaps he has *opened the seventh seal*
and there is *silence in heaven*
about the space of half an hour, and *the seventh angel*
poured out his vial into the air,
and there came a great voice
out of the temple of heaven, saying,
                         It is done.

Metaphysics

When
he gets leukemia,
he will start a collection of those little coasters
they have in bars, advertising beer,
the largest such collection in the world,
beer coasters for the *Guinness Book of Records*,
by which he will achieve some immortality,
the only kind that's really
intelligible.

Of Course

Of course,
the first philosophy
is the philosophy of the liver, the kidneys,
heart-muscle, pancreatic islets,
red bone-marrow
and stem cells,
infinite in their own fashion.

In the Socratic transplant programme,
that discourse of body, knife and electronics,
one spirit-less Self is crossed with another,
while an automatic virtuoso
plays solo violin, accompanied by an orchestra
with muted trumpets.

Mozart ought to have received a kidney,
Spinoza was waiting for new lungs
and Kierkegaard needed a heart,
or at least a valve.
All in vain.

Because
that bloody flesh
in the claws of the cave birds of narcosis
is the only wisdom –
new, real,
and transmittable.

Intensive Care Unit

God's insects stuck on pins
betrayed heroes of the abdominal cavity.

Cracked faience of whining puppets,
human soul dripping from plastic tubes.
Behind white curtains a scene
from the war of the salamanders
is endlessly getting ready.

And liturgies change
and souls change
and blushings and palenesses change
and winged prophets change
and writers of chronicles change and
gods change.

But amikacin,
the antibiotic,
is the only one.

The Birth of Sisyphus

Blood under his feet,
overhead the beating
of mother's heart.

Naked, on the naked earth.

Blood will beget a boulder,
mother will turn into a mountain.

The gods will be mad as hell,
the creed will be gone with the wind.

The birth certificate will go missing,
the nail scissors lifted by a petty thief.

In the computer a virus will bloom like a hare's-ear cabbage,
the power will be cut, Michael Jackson switched on.

Over the city, smog will sit heavy as wedding cake
and drunken shouts will stifle Solveig's song.

Global whining will be advised
and the continental plates will shift.

If an avalanche would come
the fuss would be over, but so far

it's just shift after shift,
stepping in shit,
love resembling death.

Guilty, on the guilty earth,
Sisyphus,

and what was his name again?